Getting Funded:

The Art of Writing Successful Proposals

by

George R. High

School of Urban and Public Affairs

The University of Texas at Arlington

Elements of an Effective Proposal
George R. High

The Need for an Effective Proposal

Qualified professionals frequently miss opportunities to acquire projects due to the preparation of ineffective proposals. Consequently, many projects are awarded to lesser qualified organizations and individuals. The objective of this paper is to provide an overview of the competitive bidding process and to identify elements of a successful proposal for services.

The development of an effective proposal is often *the* most important factor in the acquisition of funding for private sector, non-profit and governmental organizations. Funding can originate from federal, state and local governmental agencies, regional development organizations and international funding institutions as well as private for-profit organizations. They also can originate within multi-departmental private organizations and public agencies where there is competition for budget allocations.

The preparation of an effective proposal for services is an art in which technical elements must be accurately and succinctly conveyed in a convincing manner. Often, they are, singularly, the most important element to convince the reader that your organization is eminently qualified to undertake the sponsored project or receive funding. Therefore, it is important that organizations not only meet high technical and managerial standards but that they effectively "sell" their credentials and capabilities.

The following provides information pertaining to the competitive bidding process, elements of requests for proposals, the proposal planning process, the proposal preparation process, document preparation, and the importance of client feedback.

The Competitive Bidding Process

Although many projects are awarded as sole source, thereby circumventing the competitive bidding process, many are advertised through various mechanisms. Solicitation of small-scale services projects are typically advertised as a Request for Bid (RFB) or Request for Quotation (RFQ). Large service contracts are typically advertised as a Request for Proposal (RFP) or Request for Tender (RFT).

Requirements for bids and quotations (RFB and RFQ) generally require little more than a cost quotation; the qualifications of responding organizations are of minimal importance. Although the scope of projects which allow bidding through the RFB or RFQ process differs among agencies and organizations, they typically represent fixed-price projects of less than $10,000 value and often relate to the supply of materials, rather than services.

Service projects with fees exceeding $10,000 and originating in the United States generally are advertised as a Request for Proposal (RFP). Similar projects originating from foreign governments and international funding institutions are frequently referred to as a Request for Tender (RFT).

Requirements and guidelines to be followed in the competitive bidding process are often promulgated by legislative statutes. Such statutes define procedures to be followed to comply with funding agency regulations. In other cases, such as those from international funding organizations, the bidding process is a function of internal bidding requirements of the sponsoring organization.

Although RFP and RFT process is relatively similar among all public funding agencies, subtle differences are apparent in evaluation procedures. Bidders for large-scale projects requiring specialized services are frequently required to submit "Pre-qualifications Statements" from which a few top-ranked organizations are selected to participate in the

formal bidding process. Projects which are less specialized and generally of smaller funding amounts typically do not follow "Pre-qualifications Statement" procedures.

Use of "Pre-qualifications Statements" is beneficial to both the soliciting organization and the bidders. Bid preparation is time consuming and costly. If responding organizations can be assured that they meet minimum qualifications prior to undertaking the preparation of a formal proposal, unnecessary time and cost associated with proposal preparation by unqualified groups can be avoided. Furthermore, the evaluation of complex services proposals can be time-consuming. If unqualified bidders can be eliminated from the formal competitive bidding process, evaluation committee members can concentrate on a relatively small number of pre-qualified organizations.

The following has been prepared to define elements required for most formal competitive bids for the United States Government, the state of Texas, most international funding organizations (i.e., The World Bank and The Asian Development Bank), and many foreign governments. Although some private organizations follow similar procedures, requirements for the bidding process are generally less restrictive and uniform.

Requests for Proposals and Requests for Tenders

To the uninformed and inexperienced bidder, the competitive bidding process can be a nightmare. Solicitations received from governmental agencies frequently contain over 100 pages of technical and cost requirements and include complex certifications and representations. Although much of the material is "boiler-plate" and related to cost accounting principles and finance, it requires a great deal of time and patience to read and assimilate the material.

In nearly all cases, the competitive bidding process requires the preparation of separate cost/business and technical documents which are to be submitted in separate sealed envelopes. In all cases, bids must be received on or before specified dates and times.

Although time allotted for bid preparation differs among soliciting organizations, it seldom exceeds one month for domestic bids and two months for international bids. Actual times are dependent on requirements of the soliciting organization and the scope of the proposed project.

Cost/Business Proposal Requirements

Elements to be included in the cost/business document generally require the inclusion of key personnel proposed for the project, proposed project schedules. Other requirements for the cost/business proposal can include:

- Labor Rates (by job classification and/or individual)
- Overhead, G&A, and/or Social Charges
- Non-labor Direct Costs
- Cost Escalation Factors
- Financial Statements
- Client References

Additionally, bids for international projects frequently require inclusion of bid bonds and performance bonds. Bid bond requirements specify that the bond be forfeited if the bid is withdrawn (by the bidder) prior to contractor selection. The Bid Bond process is intended to discourage responses from contractors who are not fully committed to the project and to assure that all bids are prepared in an ethical manner. Bid bonds also tend to limit responses to organizations with sufficient financial strength to guarantee payment, should the need arise. The guarantee of payment is arranged through contractual agreement between banks working on behalf of the soliciting organization and usually totals five to ten percent of the gross amount of the bid. The source bank (working on behalf of the bidder)

charges a nominal origination fee based on a percentage of the bond amount plus interest based on amount and time.

Technical Proposal Requirements

Submittal requirements for Technical Proposals are less structured than those of Cost/Business Proposals as greater flexibility in content and presentation style is allowed; however, references to cost within the document are universally prohibited. Technical elements of an RFP generally include:

- Project Objectives and Background Information
- Scope of Work (Work Plan)
- Minimum Staff Requirements
- Minimum Facilities Requirements
- Anticipated Project Schedule and Duration
- Request for Corporate Experience
- Evaluation Criteria

Project Objectives and Background Information. A well-prepared solicitation provides a comprehensive compilation of background information and the objectives of the proposed project objectives. Although it behooves the soliciting organization to provide as much information regarding the project as possible, many solicitations only provide the Scope of Work and Project Objectives. In situations where project background information is insufficient, the responding organization must research information necessary to prepare a responsive proposal.

Minimum Staff Requirements. Minimum staff requirements are frequently included as part of a solicitation. Typically, they state minimum requirements for each of several key team members. As the proposal is developed, responding organizations are

required to provide a Curriculum Vitae (CV) or resume for each key team member. Often, the format of the CV or resume is specified, thus requiring modifications to all resumes to be submitted.

Minimum Facilities Requirements. Projects which are highly technical often require sophisticated computer hardware, computer software, laboratory and other resources. If such resources are not available through the responding organization, the bid can be considered non-responsive. In cases where required resources are not available within the organization, they often can be acquired through a third-party vendor by subcontract arrangement or through joint venture.

Anticipated Project Schedule and Duration. The anticipated project schedule and duration of the total project is often provided as part of the RFP or RFT. In many cases, the schedule is provided as well as defined task elements; in other cases, it is simply provided as total contract duration. Development of a responsive proposal generally requires an evaluation of the overall project by task and sub-task. In this manner, the project can be scheduled through discrete components which include milestones for task initiation and completion. The availability of a well-defined schedule (by task) is particularly beneficial in developing staffing requirements for the project and determining project costs.

Request for Corporate Experience. Although some solicitations do not request background information regarding the qualifications and experience of the responding organization, it should be included as part of any proposal. The inclusion of a section related to corporate experience and qualifications is important to demonstrate the capabilities of the organization to undertake and accomplish project objectives within time and cost constraints.

Evaluation Criteria. Based on previous experience, approximately 50 percent of all international Requests for Tenders include a description of the evaluation criteria to be used by the evaluation committee. Requests for Proposals issued by domestic

organizations routinely include evaluation criteria. The format of evaluation criteria listed generally states the relevant importance of various technical elements, often placing emphasis on project methodology. In some cases, the relative importance of technical and cost are stated.

In all cases in which evaluation criteria are provided, the listing is stated in relatively broad terms. Discrete elements of the criteria are not addressed, and it behooves the responding organization to determine specific elements that are significant and develop a series of criteria to use as a guide to their proposal development.

The Bid Evaluation and Selection Process

The influence of the United States Government in the bid evaluation process has filtered to many sponsoring organizations worldwide. The objectives of the evaluation process are to assure that all bid responses are evaluated without bias and that all responding organizations have an equal opportunity for contract award. The evaluation typically includes the formation of a selection committee comprised of technical, managerial and financial personnel. Proposals under review are evaluated on a variety of technical criteria (refer to Section 3.2.6) and total scores are compiled to determine rankings of each. Those organizations which rank the highest are further evaluated to determine reasonableness of cost. Final selection is often based on the relative values of technical quality vs. cost. In this manner, highly qualified technical bids may receive the award, even though proposed budgets may be higher.

Although the system should be equitable to all parties, it is frequently corrupted by subjective and "political" influences. Domestically, the process is frequently corrupted through the "good ol' boy system" to favor long-term friendships. In the international community, the process is corrupted by gratuities and bribes. This paper does not attempt to address behind-the-scenes efforts to influence decision makers, rather it is designed to present elements which lead to preparing an award-winning proposal.

Proposal Planning Process

Proposal preparation is frequently approached as a "step child" with minimal consideration given to research and present substantive material and define the true purpose of the solicitation. Furthermore, most proposals are prepared as relatively superficial technical documents rather than as a marketing or sales vehicle.

Proposal development must be approached in a structured and well organized manner. To maximize the potential for success, the process must:

- Define the Target Readers
- Define Un-stated Program Goals and Objectives
- Define the Competition (including funding limitations)
- Demonstrate Detailed Knowledge of the Subject
- Solicit and Use Input from Outside Sources
- Identify Innovative Concepts, Alternatives and Options

Define the Target Readers

Solicitations typically are prepared through the guidance of one or two key individuals within the funding organization. Assuming that such solicitations are not "tailored" to meet the qualifications of a specific contractor, they are generally presented in an objective manner. Unfortunately, the "human factor" is present in all solicitations and many are biased in favor of one or two potential contractors or organizations. Although it is seldom possible to alter biases of key individuals involved in the proposal evaluation process, the proposal author must be aware that they exist. When reader/evaluator biases are known, steps can be taken during the proposal preparation process to offset preconceived objections and to target salient elements which demonstrate a high level of responsiveness to project goals and objectives.

Therefore, an initial step in the proposal preparation process must include an identification of target readers. Knowledge of likes, dislikes and biases of selection committee members should be researched through reliable sources and information should be considered as an integral part of the proposal planning process.

Define the Program's Un-Stated Goals and Objectives

All RFP documents for domestic projects provide a section entitled "Scope of Work." In international solicitations, the section is most often entitled "Terms of Reference." Although the Scope of Work or Terms of Reference typically provide detailed information regarding the proposed project, they frequently do not provide the insight necessary for the preparation of a responsive proposal. When the true objectives of any given project are fully understood and when relevant information is available, a responsive proposal can be prepared. It behooves the responding organization to research and understand the true objectives of any project prior to preparing their proposal.

Define the Competition

Strengths and weaknesses of the competition should be assessed to determine if such organizations have a "competitive edge" for the pursuit of the subject project. A "competitive edge" may include such elements as better proximity to the work site, previous successful working relationship with the sponsoring organization, larger staff size or greater corporate resources. Although it is not possible to offset many factors, they often can be addressed in a manner to "defuse" potential objections. For example, factors relating to distance can be offset by proposing the establishment of a field office near the work site or sponsoring agency. The potential objection can be further off-set by pointing out that availability of a field office would assure that all key project team members will be fully committed to the project whereas competitor firms with local offices would have a staff which would be assigned to numerous projects.

In addition to the evaluation of the competition, the availability of funds and funding limitations should be known. Although funding limitations and budgets are often confidential, they are frequently available through informal discussions with appropriate individuals. If such sources are not available, relatively accurate cost estimates can be derived from budget information for similar projects and through pricing of elements of the proposed project. In all cases, it is important to determine your competitor's pricing scheme.

Identify Alternatives and Options

All solicitations allow for the presentation of alternative work methods. Furthermore, soliciting organizations often lack the sophistication necessary to accomplish the desired goals and objectives. As a result, proposal development should include the identification of alternative methods and concepts which can be applied to the project. Those alternatives which appear viable should be discussed to provide a means to assure the reader that the proposed work plan has been thoroughly evaluated and that all aspects of the project are fully understood.

Knowledge of the Subject

Detailed knowledge of the subject matter is paramount to the preparation of a responsive proposal. In many cases, a unique approach to a given project is warranted. New technologies which can be applied to the project must be thoroughly understood by the proposal preparation team or the individual responsible for proposal preparation to assure that they will be adequately described in the document. The proposal author must remain cognizant that many proposals are reviewed by a multi-disciplinary evaluation team and that many team members will have little or no knowledge of new technologies available and have not previously been exposed to innovative concepts in project design or management. In some cases, evaluation team members have little or no knowledge of the

goals or objectives of the project which is under consideration. Lack of knowledge of the proposed project and innovative technology presented in the proposal must be compensated through an "education" process which can only be conveyed through text, tabular and graphic format.

Solicit Input from Outside Sources

When information pertaining to the subject matter cannot be acquired from sponsoring organizations, it must be sought from other sources. Often, individuals with previous experience in the subject matter can be solicited to acquire valuable input. In some cases, published information, available through government and private sources can be used to provide background data. It is the responsibility of the proposal author (or team leader) to determine the relevancy and accuracy of third-party sources and, therefore, the use of information from such sources. Whereas some information can be extremely beneficial, reliance on incorrect information can be devastating.

Planning the Proposal Preparation Process

Appropriate and thorough planning is required to prepare an effective proposal. Elements of the planning process are:
- Proposal Strategy Development
- Outline Preparation
- Scheduling (by components)
- Assignment of Proposal Preparation Team
- Draft Reviews and Final Draft Preparation

Proposal Strategy Development

The design of the proposal strategy is often the most time consuming and important aspect of the proposal preparation process. Executing a good design requires a thorough understanding of the stated and unstated objectives of the proposed project, potential costs, technical limitations which may exist, and the development of a sound technical approach to accomplish goals and objectives.

Effective proposals are typically developed through joint input from individuals with differing technical and managerial skills. Ideas and alternative concepts are discussed among individuals and a well defined proposal strategy is developed as an amalgamation of input from all sources. It is the responsibility of the manager to filter and evaluate all concepts, determine which concepts are viable and expand on those to be addressed in the proposal. To accomplish this objective, the proposal manager must be open-minded and willing to pursue new concepts.

Outline Preparation

A tentative proposal outline is developed following input from technical, marketing and managerial team members. The outline is structured clearly to identify relevant aspects to be included in Technical and Cost/Business proposal documents. For planning purposes, the outline should be annotated to amplify significant sections; however, it must be viewed as tentative, to be used as a guideline for the preparation, rather than as an absolute format to be followed. The development of the Technical Proposal is a creative process; as such, some degree of flexibility must be allowed.

Scheduling

Preparation of a proposal for a multi-component project typically requires authorship from a variety of technical, marketing, administrative, and support individuals. To maximize use of personnel and other resources available through the organization,

sections of the Technical Proposal and elements related to cost should be developed to draw upon the talents of all individuals. Furthermore, ample time and adequate labor resources must be allocated to all aspects of proposal development (including typing, editing, printing and binding functions) to distribute the workload among all team members.

Schedule for the preparation of large-scale proposals is similar to scheduling requirements necessary for project operations. Appropriate personnel must be assigned to specific proposal elements ranging from technical writing, labor estimating and costing. Individuals should be assigned to work on proposal elements which relate to his or her specific experience and capabilities.

Scheduling also should be developed to assure that proposal deadlines are met. Experience has shown that many proposals are finalized as a "crash effort" to meet an impending deadline. As a result, the final review process is frequently circumvented and documents are issued which contain errors and omissions. To avoid the "crash effort" syndrome, deadlines for document sections and ample review and editing periods must be established. If properly scheduled, ample document preparation time also avoids the need for long hours of preparation time which leads to mistakes.

Assignment of Proposal Preparation Team

Assignment of appropriate personnel for specific proposal preparation functions is essential to assure input from specialists in various fields of study. All organizations are made up of individuals with diversified skills and capabilities and an appropriate mix of technical, managerial and clerical skills is necessary for the development of proposal documents which:

- reflect the true capabilities of the organization,
- demonstrate depth and breadth of technical expertise, and
- capitalize on the skills of the staff.

Although many technically qualified individuals have difficulty expressing their idea in writing and very few have experience in proposal preparation, they frequently are originators of innovative concepts. Proper management of the technical staff and solicitation of their input typically results in a more comprehensive and creative proposal than would be otherwise possible. A primary task of the individual responsible for proposal preparation is to assure that technical input from such individuals is clearly expressed and appropriately presented.

Proposals requiring input from a multi-disciplinary team of professionals are frequently approached on a theoretical basis as an initial step. It is the responsibility of the proposal preparation manager to transcend theoretical concepts to formulate and develop a realistic approach to the subject.

Draft Reviews and Final Draft Preparation

Appropriate planning for the proposal preparation process should allow ample time for draft document review by multiple editors. Under such circumstances, editorial reviews should:

- determine comprehensiveness of the document,
- identify weak or incomplete sections,
- identify and correct inconsistencies in approach,
- provide suggestions for improvements, and
- clarify vague proposal elements.

The review process should not be directed toward grammatical corrections or document format. Grammatical and document format editorial functions are an element of the final document preparation phase.

Final Document Preparation

The best proposal is of no value if it does not invite reading and if it is not easily understood by the evaluation committee. Furthermore, the document often serves as the only substantive exposure an organization has to the potential client thus requiring the document to succinctly convey the capabilities and professionalism of the organization. To successfully fulfill requirements of a professional presentation, the document must be:

- grammatically correct,
- accurate and consistent,
- easy to read,
- clear and concise, and
- innovative.

In addition to being accurate and thorough in its presentation, the document should have "eye appeal" to the prospective reader. Text which is lengthy and documents which lack graphics fail to hold the interest of the reader. Consequently, the evaluation of documents which fail to gain and hold the interest of the reader also fail to convey necessary information.

Proper Grammar

The need for proper grammar cannot be overstated. Although the use of idioms and colloquialisms may be acceptable to some evaluation committee members, they may not be favorably received by others. Furthermore, bids for international projects are often evaluated by individuals with limited knowledge of the English language and those unfamiliar with American idioms. The use of the "King's English" is generally understood throughout the world and should be the premise for all written communications.

Accuracy and Consistency

Accuracy of information is necessary to maintain credibility with the prospective client. Furthermore, as the proposed Scope of Work frequently becomes an integral portion of the contract for services, information presented must be accurate, consistent and free of ambiguities. Inconsistent and ambiguous information can lead to disagreements during the course of the project which ultimately result in time delays, credibility gaps and adverse impacts to project costs.

Readability

As previously referenced, a proposal must be read to be effective. In addition to the need to accurately convey all technical elements, a well-written proposal must also be formatted and presented in a manner which invites reading.

Numerous software packages are available which support sophisticated laser and multi-color plotters. The use of such packages enables text to be formatted in a wide variety of font styles and sizes which can be used to make the document unique and interesting.

Readability also can be enhanced through:
- avoidance of long and complex sentences,
- avoidance of long paragraphs,
- appropriate spacing and page margins,
- use of page breaks as section dividers, and
- use of graphics, tables and color.

The Use of Innovative Presentation Techniques

The use of innovative and creative presentation techniques contributes to the "readability" of the document. If the material prepared does not invite reading, it will not receive the attention necessary to ensure success. Furthermore, as the subject proposal

probably constitutes one of several which will be received by the sponsoring agency, careful consideration must be given to make it unique. It also must highlight important aspects which can be used to "sell" the concept and convince the reviewer that your approach to the project, methodology and qualifications will result in a superior product.

Document preparation should include use of "white space" and an easy to read format. Although such practices do not enhance the quality of the text, they tend to promote document review and evaluation.

The Final Edit

The final edit is an element of proposal preparation which is most frequently neglected. To avoid scheduling problems associated with the process, the Proposal Preparation Manager must allow sufficient time to permit document review by members of the proposal preparation team and others. Independent review by individuals not associated with the proposal is suggested to provide insight leading to the effectiveness of the document to convey the intended message. Time requirements to permit revisions in text content and document format also must be allowed.

Obtaining and Using Positive and Negative Feedback

An organization should not operate in a vacuum. Positive and negative feedback from the funding source or client organization is essential to identify proposal strengths and weaknesses to improve future proposal efforts. Mechanisms used to acquire feedback include Post-award Debriefings and the acquisition of competitive (winning) bids.

Post-award Debriefing

Knowledge of bid failures is important to the preparation of future bids. Although not routinely conducted by international funding sources, nearly all U.S. governmental

agencies are required to provide post-award debriefings to organizations which fail in the procurement process. If debriefings can be attained from international organizations, they are most often in the form of one-on-one informal discussions between key individuals of the client and submitting organizations.

Debriefings held by U.S. governmental agencies most often are held as one or more formal sessions where two or more members of both organizations are present. In all cases, debriefings include a synopsis of strengths and weaknesses of specific elements of your proposal. In some cases, it is possible to determine the relative strengths and weaknesses as compared to other bidders.

In addition to the obvious benefits derived from debriefing sessions, the submitting organization is afforded the opportunity to establish improved rapport with client evaluation team members, an opportunity to "sell" the qualifications of your organization and a sincere demonstration of interest in working with the client in the future. Therefore, it behooves members of the submitting organization to approach each debriefing session in a positive and constructive manner. Whereas elements of the evaluation may be erroneous, one must remain cognizant that misinterpretation of proposal elements by evaluation committee members also demonstrate inadequacies in the proposal document. Furthermore, as debriefings are held after a formal award has been made, a confrontational position only can serve to alienate client relationships.

Future Bids

Learn from previous mistakes
and
apply that which is learned.

Remember, life goes on — even after an unsuccessful bid!

main

336.185 HIGH
High, George R.
Getting funded

WITHDRAWN

DATE DUE	
APR 1 8 1997	MAY 1 7 2003
	JUL 2 4 2004
DEC 0 4 1998	
MAR 0 6 1999	MAY 0 2 2005
JUL 2 3 1999	NOV 2 9 2008
NOV 1 3 2002	MAR 3 1 2009
FEB 2 1 2002	
AUG 0 6 2002	
MAR 0 3 2003	